SHARKS CAN'T SMILE!

AND OTHER AMAZING FACTS

By Elizabeth Dennis
Illustrated by Lee Cosgrove

Ready-to-Read

SIMON SPOTLIGHT

An imprint of Simon & Schuster Children's Publishing Division • New York London Toronto Sydney New Delhi
1230 Avenue of the Americas, New York, New York 10020 • This Simon Spotlight edition July 2020 • Text and illustrations copyright © 2020
Simon & Schuster, Inc. Stock photos by iStock and Shutterstock. • All rights reserved, including the right of reproduction in whole or in part in any
form. SIMON SPOTLIGHT, READY-TO-READ, and colophon are registered trademarks of Simon & Schuster, Inc. • For information about special
discounts for bulk purchases, please contact Simon & Schuster Special Sales at 1-866-506-1949 or business@simonandschuster.com.
Manufactured in the United States of America 0620 LAK • 1 2 3 4 5 6 7 8 9 10 • Library of Congress Cataloging-in-Publication Data
Names: Dennis, Elizabeth, author. | Cosgrove, Lee, illustrator. Title: Sharks can't smile! : and other amazing facts / by Elizabeth Dennis;
illustrations by Lee Cosgrove. Other titles: Sharks can not smile Description: New York : Simon Spotlight, an imprint of Simon & Schuster
Children's Publishing Division, 2020. | Series: Super facts for super kids | Summary: "A nonfiction Level 2 Ready-to-Read filled with fun facts
about what makes sharks super"— Provided by publisher. Identifiers: LCCN 2019056954 | ISBN 9781534467712 (paperback) | ISBN 9781534467729
(hardcover) | ISBN 9781534467736 (eBook) Subjects: LCSH: Sharks—Miscellanea—Juvenile literature. | Children's questions and answers.
Classification: LCC QL638.9 .D457 2020 | DDC 597.3—dc23 LC record available at https://lccn.loc.gov/2019056954

GLOSSARY

cartilage: a soft material that human ears and noses, and shark skeletons, are made of

filter: to sort out

gills: organs that act as a fish's lungs and helps it breathe underwater

lateral line: a system of organs that allow sharks to sense pressure and movement in the water

plankton: tiny plants and animals that float in lakes, rivers, and oceans

predator: an animal that hunts, kills, and eats other animals

prey: an animal hunted by a predator

reef: strips of coral, rock, or sand that are located in shallow water near coasts

scales: a bony material on the outside of shark and fish bodies

skeleton: a bony structure inside humans and other animals

snout: the part of an animal's face that includes its nose, mouth, and jaws

swell: to grow bigger

Note to readers: Some of these words may have more than one definition. The definitions above match how these words are used in this book.

CONTENTS

Sharks can't smile, but can they live for hundreds of years?

How are sharks like human ears?

By the time you get to the end of this book, you'll know the answers to these questions and more about what makes sharks super!

CHAPTER 1
SHARKS, SHARKS, EVERYWHERE!

There are more than 500 different kinds of sharks. They live in every ocean in the world and in some lakes and rivers.

Sharks are often named for what makes them special.

Young tiger sharks have stripes on their skin.

Saw sharks have snouts like saws.

Carpet sharks look like carpets because they live on the ocean floor.

Blue sharks have blue skin.

Swell sharks can get bigger by swallowing water.

Sharks also come in all sizes.

American pocket sharks are shorter than a new pencil.

Whale sharks can be longer than a school bus!

American pocket shark: about five and a half inches long

new number 2 pencil: seven and a half inches long

shortfin mako shark: up to nearly 13 feet long

megamouth shark: up to 17 feet long

great white shark: up to more than 20 feet long

school bus: up to 45 feet long

whale shark: up to 59 feet long

All sharks are predators (say: PRED-uh-turz). That means they hunt and eat other animals called prey (say: PRAY). Different sharks eat different prey. Some even eat other sharks!

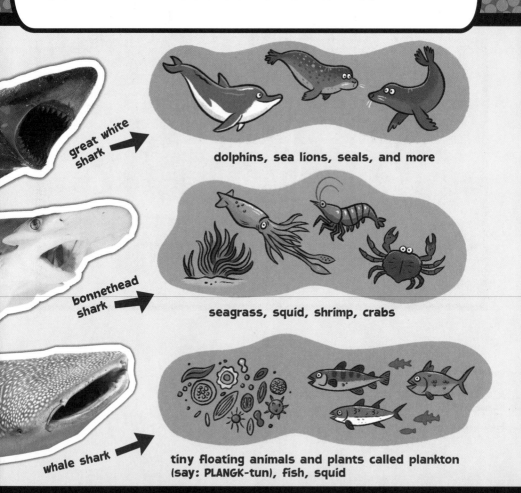

great white shark → dolphins, sea lions, seals, and more

bonnethead shark → seagrass, squid, shrimp, crabs

whale shark → tiny floating animals and plants called plankton (say: PLANGK-tun), fish, squid

Basking sharks swim with their mouths open to let in water. Then their body filters, or sorts out, the food in the water so they can eat it.

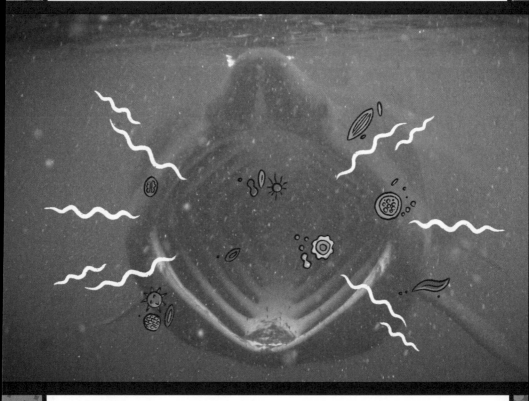

Whatever and however they eat, every shark loves a good meal!

CHAPTER 2

SHARK POWERS!

Sharks have many powers that make them special.

• Sharks breathe through gills, which are like lungs that work underwater. They have **five or more gills** on each side of their body.

• Sharks use **fins** to change direction, slow down, stay level, and more.

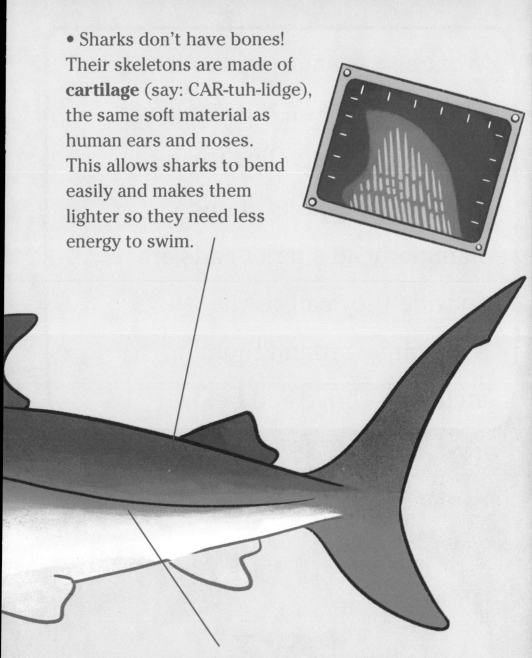

• Sharks don't have bones! Their skeletons are made of **cartilage** (say: CAR-tuh-lidge), the same soft material as human ears and noses. This allows sharks to bend easily and makes them lighter so they need less energy to swim.

• Sharks have a **lateral** (say: LAT-ur-ull) **line**, a system of organs in their body that senses pressure and movement in water.

What else is amazing about sharks? Their eyes are on the sides of their head, which lets them see in many directions at once. Hammerhead shark heads are so wide they can see in a full circle around them, including above and below!

hammerhead shark

Many sharks protect their eyes with an extra clear eyelid. Great white sharks protect their eyes by rolling them back into their head!

That's not the only cool thing about shark eyes. They also seem to glow in the dark! A layer inside shines like a mirror when light hits it. This helps sharks see ten or more times farther than humans can in low light.

BOO!

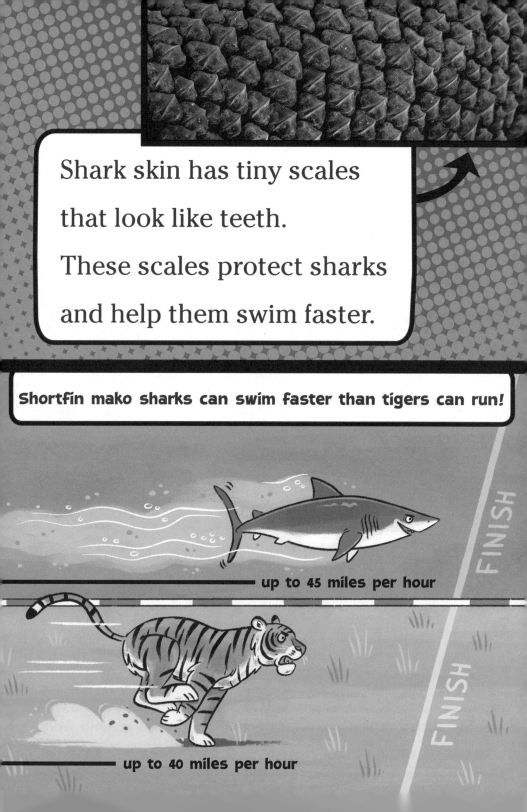

Shark skin has tiny scales that look like teeth.

These scales protect sharks and help them swim faster.

Shortfin mako sharks can swim faster than tigers can run!

up to 45 miles per hour

FINISH

up to 40 miles per hour

FINISH

What beats swimming fast?

An amazing sense of smell!

Some sharks can smell one drop of

blood in 10 billion drops of water.

That's about as many drops needed

to fill a swimming pool.

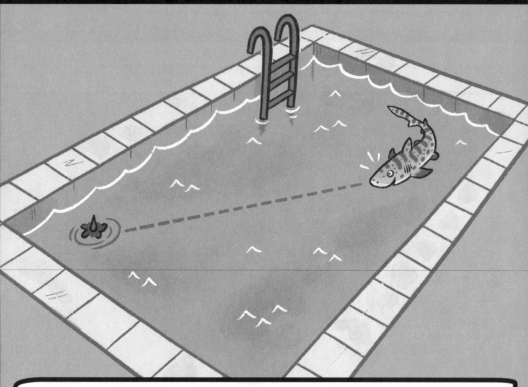

Leopard sharks know which direction a scent is coming from based on which nostril (say: NOSS-truhll) it reaches first.

Sharks also have a special sense that allows them to detect the heartbeats of nearby animals, even if the animals are hiding. How awesome is that?

CHAPTER 3

SHARKS CAN'T SMILE . . . AND OTHER STRANGE FACTS

Sharks don't have the muscles needed to smile, but if they did, they would show off many rows of teeth.

Great white sharks can grow up to 20,000 teeth in their lifetime to replace any that they lose.

Shark teeth can be long, short, wide, thin, curved, or pointy, but they are not used for chewing.

Most sharks use teeth to bite . . .

and then they swallow food whole!

sand tiger shark

basking shark

Shark teeth have a coating that keeps them from getting cavities!

Speaking of teeth, sharks can open their mouths really wide because they can move both their upper and lower jaws, unlike humans.

They often take a sample bite of prey to make sure it is good to eat.

When a shark eats something by mistake that's not food, sometimes it has a gross way of spitting it out. The shark's stomach comes out of its body through its mouth and turns inside out!

What is stranger than that?

A shark that lives forever . . . almost!

Scientists believe Greenland sharks

can live for many hundreds of years.

United States of America:
Declaration of Independence
signed in 1776

That means a Greenland shark that's alive today could have been born before the Declaration of Independence of the United States was signed on July 4, 1776!

oldest Greenland sharks: likely born long before 1776

Can you imagine living for hundreds of years and never sleeping? Well, most sharks don't sleep! They have to move forward to breathe, so they can slow down, but never completely fall asleep. Sharks also can't swim backward.

Epaulette (say: EH-puh-let) sharks have an amazing way of breathing if they get stuck on dry land or reefs.

They slow down their heart, lungs, and brain, and can live for an hour on one breath!
Then they use their fins like feet to walk back to the water!

If you could be like a shark,

would you want many rows of teeth

or to glow in the dark?

Would you want your bones to bend

like your ears do?

The coolest thing about sharks is . . . up to you!

Turn the page to learn about why we need to protect sharks!

Some people think sharks are not in danger of dying out because they are predators, but this is not true. Every year, humans kill up to 100 million sharks, often because of fishing. Sharks also get caught in fishing nets meant for other kinds of fish.

The world needs sharks to keep oceans healthy and balanced. Without sharks, their prey could take over and eat all the food in an area. Then, without any food, all the fish could die out. Without smaller fish to eat plants like algae (say: AL-jee), plants can grow so much that they block sunlight, putting animals that live in coral reefs in danger, and so on.

You can help sharks every day by using a reusable water bottle instead of plastic bottles that are only used once. A lot of plastic ends up in the ocean. It can hurt, or even kill animals if they eat or get tangled up in it. You can help by making sure to never leave trash on the beach. Keeping the ocean healthy starts with sharks . . . and you!